How t

(i) Look up the
(ii) Find the ne
this date is lis
(iii) The numb
your Mars num

if

is

...January 1950 = Mars 7;
28 October 1927 = Mars 8; 21 May 1978 = Mars 5)

Your year not listed? Sorry about that. Please write to us (enclosing SAE) and we'll let you know your sign.

1921		**1925**		**1929**		**1933**		**1937**		**1941**	
1/1	11	24/8	11	7/4	12	**1932**		**1936**		21/7	10
5/1	12	19/10	12	16/5	1	18/1	11	14/1	12	24/9	11
13/2	1	19/12	1	26/6	2	25/2	12	22/2	1	19/11	12
25/3	2			9/8	3	3/4	1	1/4	2		
6/5	3	**1925**		3/10	4	12/5	2	13/5	3	**1940**	
18/6	4	5/2	2	20/12	3	22/6	3	25/6	4	4/1	1
3/8	5	24/3	3			4/8	4	10/8	5	17/2	2
19/9	6	9/5	4	**1929**		20/9	5	26/9	6	1/4	3
6/11	7	26/6	5	10/3	4	13/11	6	14/11	7	17/5	4
26/12	8	12/8	6	13/5	5					3/7	5
		28/9	7	4/7	6	**1933**		**1937**		19/8	6
1922		13/11	8	21/8	7	6/7	7	5/1	8	5/10	7
18/2	9	28/12	9	6/10	8	26/8	8	13/3	9	20/11	8
13/9	10			18/11	9	9/10	9	14/5	8		
30/10	11	**1926**		29/12	10	19/11	10	8/8	9	**1941**	
11/12	12	9/2	10			28/12	11	30/9	10	4/1	9
		23/3	11	**1930**				11/11	11	18/2	10
1923		3/5	12	6/2	11	**1934**		21/12	12	2/4	11
21/1	1	15/6	1	17/3	12	4/2	12			16/5	12
4/3	2	1/8	2	24/4	1	14/3	1	**1938**		2/7	1
16/4	3			3/6	2	22/4	2	30/1	1		
30/5	4	**1927**		14/7	3	2/6	3	12/3	2	**1942**	
16/7	5	22/2	3	28/8	4	15/7	4	23/4	3	11/1	2
1/9	6	17/4	4	20/10	5	30/8	5	7/6	4	7/3	3
18/10	7	6/6	5			18/10	6	22/7	5	26/4	4
4/12	8	25/7	6	**1931**		11/12	7	7/9	6	14/6	5
		10/9	7	16/2	4			25/10	7	1/8	6
		26/10	8	30/3	5	**1935**		12/12	8	17/9	7
1924		8/12	9	10/6	6	29/7	8			1/11	8
19/1	9			1/8	7	16/9	9	**1939**		15/12	9
6/3	10	**1928**		17/9	8	28/10	10	29/1	9		
24/4	11	19/1	10	30/10	9	7/12	11	21/3	10	**1943**	
24/6	12	28/2	11	10/12	10			25/5	11	26/1	10

8/3	11	**1948**		**1953**		**1958**		**1963**	
17/4	12	12/2	5	8/2	1	3/2	10	3/6	6
27/5	1	18/5	6	20/3	2	17/3	11	27/7	7
8/7	2	17/7	7	1/5	3	27/4	12	12/9	8
24/8	3	3/9	8	14/6	4	7/6	1	25/10	9
		17/10	9	29/7	5	21/7	2	5/12	10
1944		26/11	10	14/9	6	21/9	3		
28/3	4			1/11	7	28/10	2	**1964**	
22/5	5	**1949**		20/12	8			13/1	11
12/7	6	4/1	11			**1959**		20/2	12
29/8	7	11/2	12	**1954**		10/2	3	29/3	1
13/10	8	21/3	1	9/2	9	10/4	4	7/5	2
25/11	9	30/4	2	12/4	10	1/6	5	17/6	3
		10/6	3	3/7	9	20/7	6	30/7	4
1945		23/7	4	24/8	10	5/9	7	15/9	5
5/1	10	7/9	5	21/10	11	21/10	8	6/11	6
14/2	11	27/10	6	4/12	12	3/12	9		
25/3	12	26/12	7					**1965**	
2/5	1			**1955**		**1960**		29/6	7
11/6	2	**1950**		15/1	1	14/1	10	20/8	8
23/7	3	28/3	6	26/2	2	23/2	11	4/10	9
7/9	4	11/6	7	11/4	3	2/4	12	14/11	10
12/11	5	10/8	8	26/5	4	11/5	1	23/12	11
26/12	4	25/9	9	11/7	5	20/6	2		
		6/11	10	27/8	6	2/8	3	**1966**	
1946		15/12	11	13/10	7	21/9	4	30/1	12
22/4	5			29/11	8			9/3	1
20/6	6	**1951**				**1961**		17/4	2
9/8	7	22/1	12	**1956**		6/5	5	28/5	3
24/9	8	1/3	1	14/1	9	29/6	6	11/7	4
6/11	9	10/4	2	28/2	10	17/8	7	25/8	5
17/12	10	21/5	3	15/4	11	1/10	8	12/10	6
		4/7	4	3/6	12	13/11	9	4/12	7
1947		18/8	5	6/12	1	24/12	10		
25/1	11	5/10	6					**1967**	
4/3	12	24/11	7	**1957**		**1962**		12/2	8
12/4	1			28/1	2	2/2	11	31/3	7
21/5	2	**1952**		17/3	3	12/3	12	19/7	8
1/7	3	20/1	8	4/5	4	19/4	1	10/9	9
13/8	4	27/8	9	21/6	5	29/5	2	23/10	10
1/10	5	12/10	10	8/8	6	9/7	3	1/12	11
1/12	6	21/11	11	24/9	7	22/8	4		
		30/12	12	8/11	8	12/10	5	**1968**	
				23/12	9			9/1	12

17/2	1		
28/3	2		
8/5	3		
21/6	4		
5/8	5		
21/9	6		
9/11	7		
29/12	8		
1969			
25/2	9		
21/9	10		
4/11	11		
15/12	12		
1970			
24/1	1		
7/3	2		
18/4	3		
2/6	4		
18/7	5		
3/9	6		
20/10	7		
6/12	8		
1971			
23/1	9		
12/3	10		
3/5	11		
6/11	12		
26/12	1		
1972			
10/2	2		
27/3	3		
12/5	4		
28/6	5		
15/8	6		
1/10	7		
15/11	8		
30/12	9		
1973			
12/2	10		

26/3	11
8/5	12
20/6	1
12/8	2
30/10	1
24/12	2

1974

27/2	3
20/4	4
9/6	5
27/7	6
12/9	7
28/10	8
10/12	9

1975

21/1	10
3/3	11
11/4	12
21/5	1
1/7	2
14/8	3
17/10	4
25/11	3

1976

18/3	4
16/5	5
7/7	6
24/8	7
8/10	8
21/11	9

1977

1/1	10
9/2	11
20/3	12
27/4	1
6/6	2
17/7	3
1/9	4
26/10	5

1978

26/1	4
10/4	5
14/6	6
4/8	7
19/9	8
2/11	9
12/12	10

1979

20/1	11
27/2	12
7/4	1
16/5	2
26/6	3
8/8	4
24/9	5
19/11	6

1980

12/3	5
4/5	6
10/7	7
29/8	8
12/10	9
22/11	10
30/12	11

1981

6/2	12
17/3	1
25/4	2
5/6	3
18/7	4
2/9	5
21/10	6
16/12	7

1982

3/8	8
20/9	9
31/10	10
10/12	11

1983

17/1	12
25/2	1
5/4	2
16/5	3
29/6	4
13/8	5
30/9	6
18/11	7

1984

11/1	8
17/8	9
5/10	10
15/11	11
25/12	12

1985

2/2	1
15/3	2
26/4	3
9/6	4
25/7	5
10/9	6
27/10	7
14/12	8

1986

2/2	9
28/3	10
9/10	11
26/11	12

1987

8/1	1
20/2	2
5/4	3
21/5	4
6/7	5
22/8	6
8/10	7
24/11	8

1988

8/1	9
22/2	10
6/4	11
22/5	12
13/7	1
25/10	12
31/10	1

1989

19/1	2
11/3	3
29/4	4
16/6	5
3/8	6
19/9	7
4/11	8
18/12	9

1990

29/1	10
11/3	11
20/4	12
31/5	1
12/7	2
31/8	3
14/12	2

1991

20/1	3
3/4	4
26/5	5
15/7	6
1/9	7
16/10	8
29/11	9

1992

9/1	10
18/2	11
28/3	12
5/5	1
14/6	2
26/7	3
12/9	4

1993

27/4	5
23/6	6
12/8	7
27/9	8
9/11	9
20/12	10

1994

28/1	11
7/3	12
14/4	1
23/5	2
3/7	3
16/8	4
4/10	5
12/12	6

1995

22/1	5
25/5	6
21/7	7
7/9	8
20/10	9
30/11	10

1996

8/1	11
15/2	12
24/3	1
2/5	2
12/6	3
25/7	4
9/9	5
30/10	6

1997

3/1	7
8/3	6
19/6	7
14/8	8
28/9	9
9/11	10
18/12	11

1998

25/1	12
4/3	1
13/4	2
24/5	3
6/7	4
20/8	5
7/10	6
27/11	7

1999

26/1	8
6/5	7
5/7	8
2/9	9
17/10	10
26/11	11

2000

4/1	12
12/2	1
23/3	2
3/5	3
16/6	4
1/8	5
17/9	6
4/11	7
23/12	8

2001

14/2	9
8/9	10
27/10	11
8/12	12

2002

18/1	1
1/3	2
13/4	3
28/5	4
13/7	5
29/8	6
15/10	7
1/12	8

You share your Mars sign with these famous people:

Ursula Andress, Clint Eastwood, Xaviera Hollander, Norman Mailer, Prince, Simone Signoret, Oliver Reed, Monica Seles, Orson Welles, Sarah Miles, Tyra Banks, Michael Bolton, Celeste Holm, Kelsey Grammer, Franco Nero, Kurt Russell and Lauryn Hill

♥♥♥♥♥♥♥♥♥♥♥♥♥♥♥♥♥♥♥♥♥♥♥

For you the pursuit of love and romance is nothing less than a personal mission—or a rampage! Your lovers must also have some get-up-and-go, or you'll get-up-and-leave! You are turned on by those who are trail blazers, tough competitors and winners. For you, it's all about mind blowing attraction, and you are excited by the prospect of hot sex anywhere and anytime! You enjoy the chase, so others must not be too eager or give in too quickly. You are a dynamic person keen to express yourself strongly in and out of the bedroom, but since you're easily bored, you will look elsewhere if a partner cannot keep up with the daredevil pace you set. Potential partners have to be decisive, independent types who are able to take care of themselves (and willing, when you let them, to take care of you, too). You're not interested in lovers with inhibitions or a reluctance to have sex with you—morning, noon and night!

You have a direct and combative temperament that needs to sort out problems head-on, particularly if you sniff subterfuge or deceit. You hate lies and loathe false promises. Never afraid of confrontation, you love a feisty argument, especially if it clears the air. Your temper can flare up quickly, particularly if you've been ignored or insulted. Arguments can seem like a no-holds barred contest, but you forgive quickly and enjoy making-up. On a more serious note, we've found some born with this Mars placement who seem to attract brutes or overly aggressive types. If you ever feel the urge to strike out yourself, we suggest you invest in a punch bag and make use of that excellent (and lethal) aim of yours!

Some Sexy Scenarios...

♥ Enjoying the risky quickie in places where you just might get caught
♥ Having a head massage to cool you down between those steamy sessions
♥ Reliving your adventurous youth and romping in the car (when parked, please!)
♥ Enjoying sports and fitness routines with partners—
you know it keeps the blood pumping

♪ Holding Out For A Hero/Living La Vida Loca ♪

Being so impulsive and courageous, you believe in the direct approach when pursuing others—there isn't much subtlety in anything you do! There's little doubt in others' minds as to whether or not you find them attractive. Equally obvious will be your displeasure at having any romantic trophy slip through your fingers. There's something of the Tarzan and Jane story in your sex life—or maybe it's the rugged and unstoppable Indiana Jones you model yourself on. But beware that your actions don't intimidate potential partners—others can wither just thinking about you! Right from the start you want to be proud of your partner—but bear in mind that pride sometimes comes before a fall! At times you try to prove yourself through your sexual prowess and think your performance is a measure of your self-worth. The slightest hint of rejection or disinterest from a partner, however special they are, can have you re-evaluating your every move. Getting involved long-term is a challenge because you need to watch out for that selfish, me-first and combative streak (the Sondheim song *Being Alive* best describes what you need). You need a gutsy partner who will appreciate your childlike qualities and contagious enthusiasm... challenging and driving each other on will be bliss.

Road to Glory/Road to Oblivion

Others should:
- let you make the first move so you feel you're still in charge
- keep you guessing, chasing and laughing; compete but let you win
- be independent but vulnerable enough to need your protection
- arouse you physically and fire you up mentally

Others should avoid:
- trying to make you jealous
- playing too hard to get—for you, it's only fun for a while!
- bossing you around or trying to fit you into their routines
- criticising your actions or siding with your 'enemies'

Hot dates

2000: 1 August to 17 September; 24 September to 19 October; 4 November to 23 December
2001: 7 November to 2 December
2002: 18 January to 1 March; 13 July to 29 August; 8 September to 9 October; 15 October to 7 January 2003

You share your Mars sign with these famous people:

Muhammad Ali, Lucille Ball, Tom Cruise, Bette Davis, Robert DeNiro, John Derek, Glenda Jackson, Eartha Kitt, Mick Jagger, John F. Kennedy, Michael Jackson, Madonna, Mariah Carey, Courteney Cox, Lucy Lawless, Bruce Willis and Christine Keeler

♥♥♥♥♥♥♥♥♥♥♥♥♥♥♥♥♥♥♥♥♥

This is a truly sensual and lusty position for Mars, and potential lovers must be able to turn on all five of your senses. You are motivated to find a stable union with someone who makes you feel safe and takes care of you through thick and thin. You seek practical and reliable partners who understand the value of everything. Most romantic set-ups suit you so long as they provide all those creature comforts you desire. Your investment of energy in securing a comfortable lifestyle is coupled with strong physical needs and a tremendous appetite for sex. Sexually, you prefer a comfortable setting with music, wine, candles and, of course, an attentive, considerate partner who appreciates your stamina. Feeling more at one with nature than most, you'll find enormous sexual stimulation in the great outdoors. It won't be much of a leap for you to move from a domestic sexual scenario to the garden!

It takes one hell of a lot to get you truly angry, but once you do, heaven help us! You hate losing control of your temper and fear the beast within may show itself! If pushed to the limit, you are likely to wipe your opponent out with one fell swoop. You fight back with stubborn resistance that's grounded in an unshakeable belief in your own convictions—you always have the final word. You are most unforgiving when taken advantage of or if someone lets you down—to you, this is total betrayal of trust. It takes you a long time to get over such outrage, and once you've forgiven you are unlikely ever to forget. You come down hard on irresponsible people—those who would rather slack off than tackle an honest day's work are like a red rag to a bull for you!

Some Sexy Scenarios...
- ♥ Making love in breathtaking outdoor locations
- ♥ Letting it all hang out—going 'au naturel' (around the house, anyway)
- ♥ Trying out scenes from the movie $9^{1/2}$ Weeks—especially the food one!
- ♥ Making sure your lover pays special attention to your neck and throat
- ♥ Taking time to perfect those oral arts

♪ Biding My Time ♪

So, how do you pursue others? Well, you're not a person who likes to rush anything. You understand, as the song goes, that you just can't hurry love! You like to take your time, enjoy the moment and know that all good things come to those who wait. You are blessed with the patience of a saint and your sense of timing serves you well as you pursue others with long-term prospects in mind. You might worry too much about material security before settling down. Financial independence will help you avoid settling for second best or compromising those strong beliefs and values. You hate admitting to mistakes and once your mind's made up you are stubborn enough to continue along the same path regardless. Sometimes sour relationships continue out of loyalty, at other times from sheer possessiveness. You expect lovers to appreciate you for the care and attention you give them. Without feedback and reassurance, you could certainly start out slow and then... peter out! You hate games and uncertainty—they make you insecure and jealous. Sensibly you seek a partner who you can depend on, preferring to settle for the safe bet. Your need for powerful sexual chemistry, bolstered by your reliable animal instincts, means that you know early on whether or not there's real potential in any partnership.

Road to Glory/Road to Oblivion

Others should:
- be loyal, reliable and seeking commitment
- be able to match your sensuality and endurance
- be able to engage all your senses
- respect your beliefs and strong opinions

Others should avoid:
- indiscreet behaviour or divulging your pillow talk
- attempting to push or rush you into ANYTHING
- fickle actions
- borrowing money and not returning it

Hot dates

2000: 17 September to 13 November; 3 December to 14 February 2001
2001: 26 November to 26 December
2002: 1 March to 13 April; 29 August to 15 October; 19 November to 17 January 2003

You share your Mars sign with these famous people:

Antonio Banderas, James Cagney, Fabio, Julio Iglesias, John McEnroe, Eva Peron, Diana Ross, OJ Simpson, Barbra Streisand, Tim Allen, Irene Cara, Naomi Campbell, Sandra Bullock, Daniel Day Lewis, Hugh Grant, Sean Penn, Julianna Margulies, Courtney Love, Spike Lee and Jerry Springer

♥♥♥♥♥♥♥♥♥♥♥♥♥♥♥♥♥♥♥♥♥♥♥

You're excited by a lively debate, repartee and, yes, the titillation of phone-sex! Someone who matches your quick-witted mind and has a head full of entertaining trivia will turn you on for life. Did we say 'for life'? Sorry, we mean that they'll keep you interested for as long as they can sustain the high level of mental stimulation you require. You have to look forward to something new every week—so some would call you fickle. Be innovative like the spouses in Harold Pinter's 'The Lover', who kept the spark in their marriage by having the husband leaving the house in the morning and returning later transformed into the extramarital lover. You enjoy sex talk, especially clever innuendo, so lovers would be wise to turn you on when travelling home from work via that ever so useful mobile phone. You have a passion for sexual theories (bless those Nancy Friday books!) and discussions about every conceivable sexual scenario are almost as good as the real thing—perhaps even better?

You fight back with your tongue when others have the gall to attack you or criticise your actions. You certainly know all about fighting talk, and that sharp tongue has been known to kill at twenty paces! You have a political mind and can be a skilled tactician. Anyone wanting to argue had better know their facts and have their wits about them—as well as a packed suitcase in case you really lay their shortcomings on the line. For you, words are the most effective weapon—and others have the scars to prove it. You can see through emotional manipulation and are quick to put a stop to it. It'll be a cold day in hell when someone gets away with justifying their deceit or infidelity with lame excuses!

Some Sexy Scenarios...
♥ Trying the great seduction scene over the phone
♥ Chatting up that friendly-looking stranger on the train
♥ Writing lots of sexy (and funny) love letters
♥ Keeping those sensitive and skillful hands busy
♥ Running your own chat-line service

♪ Forever Young ♪

Oh dear—is it true? Do you think a conversation is really a contest in which the first person to draw a breath is declared the listener? You are tough to top with your sparkling quick-fire conversation, and you're certainly quick off the mark with an amusing anecdote or a sarcastic retort. As an expert at the chat-up line, you entice your objects of desire with silver tongued charm. Some love it, others want to put a lid on it or sock you in the mouth. Dump the detractors and enjoy those who love puns, quirky humour and gossip. You have an eternal curiosity about people, facts and life in general. You need to communicate verbally with a lover, so the strong, silent type ain't for you! Knowing that your mind is one of your best features, you're more than happy to exercise it and show it off. We know most of you could talk for your country—is it any surprise that you engage others with dazzling dialogue? Anyway, you sometimes feel that sex is overrated. It's the communication before, during and after sex that really does it for you—that's the most potent aphrodisiac. You're happy to be footloose and fancy free and would never attempt to tie others down (well, we won't rule that out behind closed doors!). You're in constant pursuit of youthful experiences and recognise you're only as young as the *person* you feel!

Road to Glory/Road to Oblivion

Others should:
- keep you feeling young
- appreciate your humour, wit and grasp of a variety of subjects
- tease, flirt and play Devil's advocate
- be versatile in and out of the bedroom

Others should avoid:
- giving emotionally-draining monologues
- possessive behaviour and monopolising you at social events
- having telephones engaged or mobile phones switched off!
- getting stuck in a professional or personal rut

Hot dates

2000: 4 November to 10 January 2001
2001: 14 February to 10 May; 20 July to 8 September; 15 December to 19 January 2002
2002: 13 April to 28 May; 15 October to 1 December; 8 to 31 December

You share your Mars sign with these famous people:

Tom Jones, Dolly Parton, Divine, Jane Powell, Jane Russell, Nancy Reagan, Jane Wyman, Diana Rigg, Paula Yates, Audrey Hepburn, Isabelle Adjani, Vivien Leigh, Liza Minnelli, Richard Gere, George Lucas, Alanis Morissette, Eddie Murphy, Eileen Brennan and Keanu Reeves

♥♥♥♥♥♥♥♥♥♥♥♥♥♥♥♥♥♥♥♥♥

It's really quite simple to describe people who have this Mars sign, but living with them is another matter altogether! You are not aggressive and you are not overly demanding. But what you need desperately is security, pure loyalty... AND someone who understands and connects with your complex range of emotions. You want to be an achiever in the outside world, but are torn between your goals and your devotion to home or family. For you, the inner world—be it in your own mind or within four walls—is the safest and most interesting space. You want someone considerate and needy to share that space: considerate because you experience a dozen different emotional states a day; and needy because you take great pleasure in mothering others and attending to their physical and emotional requirements. You are naturally defensive, but when you do surrender to your partner, you bring an intensity and emotionality to your mating that is simply exquisite.

You are at your most vulnerable (and dangerous) when your security and home life are threatened. When attacked, you resort to extremes: either retreating into your shell or coming out snapping and sniping. You hide your sensitivity underneath a prickly exterior, so others may avoid taking you on anyway, especially when they realise that your resentment can last a long time. Although family members comes first, they are often the ones who bear the brunt of your temper and mood swings. You do, however, defend them to the death, or unite them against a common enemy if attacked. You guard against intrusion and abhor insensitive folk who don't respect your privacy. You respond to rejection by being manipulative ("I can't go on anymore"), then by being glum, and finally wallowing in anger.

Some Sexy Scenarios...
♥ Savouring kisses and caresses under a moonlit sky
♥ Spending long winter nights in a four-poster bed in someone's ancestral home
♥ Feeling truly sexy and making the most of that cleavage
♥ Feasting on oysters and other aphrodisiacs

♪ Bridge Over Troubled Water ♪

Self-protective by nature, your sensitive streak comes to the fore when approaching new relationships. Yours is not an obvious operation—sideways like a crab you move towards your target—and it takes a while for anyone to realise your intentions. You are wary of showing too much emotion before you have proof of a potential partner's feelings—you strongly fear betrayal and can worry yourself sick. You plot carefully to avoid disappointment, are not averse to scheming, and your tenacity makes you difficult to resist. Once you've set your heart on a lover, they could face one problem: you want to pamper and nurture them forever, and never let go! Partners who need some breathing space have to contend with your tight grip. A satisfactory sex life makes you feel safe. Unable to separate your feelings from your body, you're not the best to reason with! You are highly tuned to changes in atmosphere and usually know when there's a storm brewing. If anyone's in trouble, you're the Samaritan-next-door with a helping hand. As well as nurturing, you need to be nurtured. What could be nicer than a warm and sympathetic shoulder for those days when living is painful. However streetwise and capable you may appear in other areas, when it comes to your romantic life you walk the old-fashioned path—it has to be flowers, sentimental notes, and genuine declarations of undying love.

Road to Glory/Road to Oblivion

Others should:
- always remember every type of anniversary
- nurture you; keep you safe and secure—physically & emotionally
- take your moods into account; allow you time to be alone
- remember the way to your heart is through your stomach

Others should avoid:
- being critical of your home or family
- presuming intimacy before you've decided to let them in
- being a social butterfly; you want a homebody
- asking you to choose between home and work

Hot dates

2000: 16 June to 1 August; 8 December to 14 February 2001
2001: 6 February to 17 March; June to July; 8 September to 27 October
2002: 19 January to 12 February; 28 May to 13 July; 1 December to 17 January 2003

You share your Mars sign with these famous people:

Brigitte Bardot, Boy George, Harrison Ford, Jodie Foster, Goldie Hawn, Joanna Lumley, Bette Midler, Demi Moore, Robert Redford, Cher, Kenny Rogers, Sylvester Stallone, Sting, Gillian Anderson, Toni Braxton, Ralph Fiennes, Andrew Lloyd Webber and George Clooney

♥♥♥♥♥♥♥♥♥♥♥♥♥♥♥♥♥♥♥♥♥♥

You're a big kid at heart: playful, fun and humorous (not to mention petulant and a first-class prima donna!). Sex must be entertaining, pleasurable and adventurous. You love bold and passionate people who share your sense of drama. Indeed, sex is like a stage play for you, with the goal of a standing ovation if the set is well-hung, the audience appreciative, and the actors efficient enough to remember their moves and deliver with conviction. Well, forget the ovation, some of you demand a standing ovulation! You desire someone who will put you at the centre of their world, make you feel alive, glamorous and very special indeed. You also need someone to adore and who will admire you royally in return. You have a strong desire for a larger-than-life lover with whom you can take central roles in the most romantic and dazzling soap opera ever. Lights! Camera! Action!

Partners who have managed to offend you will be subjected to a right royal sulk. You are unlikely to lash out crudely—that sort of behaviour is too obvious and quite undignified! Actually you'd rather people don't know you care enough to strike back. You have stronger pride than most and take negative remarks as personal criticism. But when you feel safe in a relationship, you can let out a booming, dramatic roar worthy of any operatic diva. If others can't spot your sensitivity underneath all that bravado, it's their loss! When hurt or if not paid enough attention, you can condescend until the cows come home. The worst crime against you is for others not to take you seriously. How can people have the audacity to survive without your golden presence?

Some Sexy Scenarios...
- ♥ On a romantic holiday in warmer climes with plenty of sex in the sun
- ♥ Being brave by admitting that voyeurism and exhibitionism have their place
- ♥ Considering making (and starring in) that risqué home video
- ♥ Indulging yourself with leisurely back rubs

♪ Let Me Entertain You ♪

One of your greatest talents is your ability to inspire others to follow you and your quest in life, without a moment's hesitation. Others are naturally drawn to you (obviously recognising your superiority without you having to spell it out!). You don't need to go to inordinate lengths to pursue those who take your fancy. You are also aware that the key to winning your prize is to be nonchalant—some people are lucky enough to get away with playing hard to get! Once you have won the object of your desire, however, you go out of your way to impress them! Extravagant gestures and surprises delivered on a grand-scale are your best methods to fuel the flames of passion—and you do it with such panache. How could anyone turn you down? How could they resist basking in the warmth of your generous attentions? You are well aware that taking care of your appearance with classy clothes and eye catching hair styles are two ways to attract your mate. Have you considered that you may be even more appealing if you occasionally expose your vulnerabilities (or, dare we say it, admit you need as much guidance as anyone else)? One piece of advice: beware of always hogging the limelight or dominating the scene with monologues—"That's enough about me. Let's talk about you... what do you think of me?"

Road to Glory/Road to Oblivion

Others should:
- be content to point the spotlight firmly in your direction
- display passion, humour and sparkle (but shine less than you)
- listen to and respect your opinions
- feed you with sincere compliments (and a few luxuries)

Others should avoid:
- taking overt control; you must *think* you're in charge!
- neglecting or ignoring you; you have a fragile ego
- meanness or criticising your generosity towards everyone
- taking credit for your success; showing-off at your expense

Hot dates

2000: 31 July to 17 September
2001: 3 January to 2 February; 14 February to 10 May;
20 July to 8 September; 27 October to 8 December
2002: 12 February to 8 March; 11 to 29 March; 13 July to 29 August

You share your Mars sign with these famous people:

Charles Bronson, Michael Caine, Joan Collins, Matt Damon, Johnny Depp, Tim Henman, Don Johnson, Joan Rivers, Peter Sellers, Cameron Diaz, Calista Flockhart, Elizabeth Hurley, Gwyneth Paltrow, Will Smith, Kevin Spacey and George Michael

♥♥♥♥♥♥♥♥♥♥♥♥♥♥♥♥♥♥♥♥♥♥♥

You're an interesting mix of earthy sensuality and practicality, so you know that there's an obstacle to your every romantic goal. That obstacle is imperfection, but you strive to find (and be) the perfect lover anyway. Finding someone who is as much a perfectionist as you and who excels in the art of 'getting it right'—including sex—is an exciting prospect, and you are diligent in your pursuit of this. Partners who are health-conscious or perhaps interested in healing therapies make you tick too. You are turned off by those who aren't concerned with self improvement or who blame others for their lack of achievement. Hygiene is a concern in sex, but it's just one manifestation of the sense of order you are always seeking. Nevertheless, you can surprise your lovers by getting down and dirty when aroused. There's a raunchy side to you that other people rarely see, and you have no qualms—when it feels right—about getting to grips with adventurous sexual techniques and, of course, practising the Kama Sutra.

People who disrupt your life and routine meet your pedantic, officious side. Nagging is the sport for which you could win Olympic Gold. Lateness, carelessness and rudeness are your pet peeves. At times, you're quite formidable; others had better keep out of your way when you're ready to nit-pick! You can be brutal with criticism, tearing others apart with pointed accusations that hit home. What they don't realise is that you save the harshest criticism for yourself. That's bad enough, but when others poke fun at your conscientious, measured approach, you can quickly turn tetchy.

Some Sexy Scenarios...
♥ Working up a sweat on an exercise programme *together*
♥ Letting rip your unbridled passion between perfectly laundered sheets
♥ Updating that childhood game of 'doctors and nurses'
♥ Plotting on paper your perfect seduction scene

♪ It's Got To Be... Perfect ♪

You're fussy and particular so you plan your romantic moves with a great attention to detail—seduction for you is an act of tactical genius. You don't mind waiting until Mr or Ms Right comes along and some of you can endure long periods of abstinence. You strive to be a skilled and attentive lover so you want appreciation of your craft from the right person! You collect information and put theory into practice to improve every sexual experience. It's all about doing a good job and you intend to provide a helpful service! You put time into relationships, and the planning of appropriate settings for romance is a skill you intend to perfect. So whether it's the dinner that you lovingly prepared or knowing just how to relieve the tension in your partner's body, you'll aim to be the best at it. At times it may seem as though you try too hard to get things right, so relaxing more and releasing your anxieties about the outcome could really boost your sex life. You tend to struggle with your highly logical and orderly approach to intimacy, so may need to shed some inhibitions by becoming more spontaneous. Deep down, you crave a relationship that doesn't require so much damn-hard work to maintain it. So take a gamble, stop analysing every nuance and throw away your 'how to' manual. No need to worry—just begin applying the things you already know so well.

Road to Glory/Road to Oblivion

Others should:
- appreciate your thoughtfulness and attention to detail
- challenge you mentally—engaging both body and mind
- understand (or ignore) your obsessive-compulsive side!
- be sexy but not sluttish!

Others should avoid:
- embarrassing you in public
- undermining your confidence
- messing up your schedule
- causing chaos in the kitchen

Hot dates

2000: 17 September to 4 November
2001: 2 February to 8 March; 6 April to 6 June; 8 September to 27 October; 8 December to 18 January 2002
2002: 29 March to 13 April; 29 August to 15 October

You share your Mars sign with these famous people:

Pamela Anderson, Sonny Bono, Richard Branson, Bill Clinton, Tori Amos, Lyle Lovett, Ethan Hawke, Leona Helmsley, Joan Crawford, Margaret Thatcher, Whitney Houston, Mary Tyler Moore, Barry White Freddie Mercury, Elvis Presley, Kim Basinger, Nicole Kidman and Lisa Kudrow

♥♥♥♥♥♥♥♥♥♥♥♥♥♥♥♥♥♥♥♥♥♥♥

Ah, those fine wines, fashionable restaurants, sophisticated music and manners from heaven! You are turned on by style, etiquette and beautiful surroundings. Pushy, rude and obtrusive people aren't welcome in your sphere! But wait, there's another side to you (especially the women). You are aroused by sparky arguments and stimulating discussion. You thrive on debate, as long as you win the most points in the end! Defending your rights and opinions really excites you, particularly between the sheets. Shame on those who think you're a pushover because you are sweet-talking, charming and polite. Your Mars placement is surely the iron fist in the velvet glove— so others won't have you figured out straightaway. Men with this Mars find arguments make steamy foreplay too, but tend to resort (and succumb) to seduction and softer tactics. Both sexes have a weakness for the divine body and stylish taste in clothes.

Your main pet hate is injustice—whether it's intolerance or an imbalance in a romantic liaison. Being so agreeable, others try to take liberties. You're not always direct ("I'm going to be assertive—if that's okay with you"), but nevertheless get what you want by using more subtle manoeuvres (usually involving flattery). You can be so disarming that for others to argue against your point may seem petty or unnecessarily personal. How can anyone win when you don't fight fair! You hate irrational behaviour and unruly outbursts, preferring to handle problems with cool, reasoned argument. If there is difficulty expressing your anger, find time to discuss your problems with an objective third party.

Some Sexy Scenarios...
♥ Making every holiday as special (and sexy) as a honeymoon
♥ Treating yourself to the most seductive and exclusive underwear
♥ Achieving the perfect balancing act by playing naked *Twister*!
♥ Enjoying those sexy bottom-hugging outfits!

♪ I'm Gonna Make You Love Me ♪

Once you've made up your mind (easier said than done!), you pour tremendous energy into developing a partnership, and excel at all aspects of romancing. You are particularly aware that being such a good listener has enormous pulling power. You pursue and seduce your mate by showering them with gifts and treats—less fortunate suitors have to settle for tactful (no!) thank you notes. When your pocket permits, you entertain with elegance whatever the expense—co-ordinating an evening out with effortless flair. You are the most attentive lover because you really want to please and in effect will do anything to keep your partner happy. Like a flattering mirror, you only reflect the other person's best side. So strong is your need for approval that in the early stages you instantly consider changing your lifestyle to fit in with your mate's. When lovers ask, "What do you need?" you reply by asking them the same question. Don't lose sight of what is important to YOU. Let's not forget the potency of that persuasive side to your nature—you sure know how to wrap others around your little finger. When lovers are in doubt, you know how to convince them they'd be better off remaining with you. As relationships are your holy grail, many of you achieve your personal ambitions and status through an enduring marriage.

Road to Glory/Road to Oblivion

Others should:
- compliment you as much as you do them
- include you in all decision-making (even if they have to make the final choice!)
- enjoy adult discussions without becoming *over*-heated
- believe in equality in the relationship

Others should avoid:
- making critical comments about your appearance
- deferring all decisions to you or refusing to argue
- criticising your taste or calling you a snob
- ugly scenes or embarrassing you with uncouth behaviour

Hot dates

2000: 4 November to 23 December
2001: 21 April to 6 May; 6 June to 5 July; 27 October to 8 December
2002: 18 January to 1 March; 1 to 30 April; 15 October to 1 December

You share your Mars sign with these famous people:

Kurt Cobain, Leonardo DiCaprio, Diana Dors, Larry Flynt, Mel Gibson, Jimi Hendrix, Grace Kelly, Rock Hudson, kd lang, Bruce Lee, Charlie Sheen, Jennifer Aniston, Mary J. Blige, Calvin Klein, Christie Brinkley, Deepak Chopra, Matt LeBlanc, Liam Neeson and LeAnn Rimes

♥♥♥♥♥♥♥♥♥♥♥♥♥♥♥♥♥♥♥♥♥♥♥

Amongst the most erotically charged of all Mars signs, it's all or nothing for you—forget lukewarm relationships, half-hearted sex and lovers who have little under the surface. You are driven to explore and penetrate all aspects of your potential life-mate. You also thrive on testing your limits—physically and emotionally—and seek out mates who show signs of being receptive to your extreme appetite. Some of you view sex as all-important, so much so that it can sometimes lead to anguish—or addiction! The darker side of your passion ranges from an overpowering jealousy to an urge to act upon even your taboo desires. You are turned on by sexually powerful, intriguing and intense personalities. Although always excited by the chase, ultimately you are looking for a profound and lasting union. On this deeper level, you are motivated to transcend the purely animal, physical act to reach a mystical sexual and emotional bond.

Acts of treachery turn you from burning passion to (apparent) freezing indifference. Sarcasm can be a biting weapon to cut down disloyal lovers swiftly. When reproached by others, you retaliate with stinging accuracy. Yes, you can be vindictive—having sussed the other person's weak spots, you know exactly where to aim for maximum effect! When betrayed you can fight dirty and use devious tactics—this is, we know, often done in defence of your super-sensitive side. At other times you are an enigma, walking away from a fight. You can leave enemies bewildered; they don't know if they have hurt you—or whether you'll be back to even the score! Your extreme, do-or-die personality always provokes strong reactions. You never forget the smallest treachery and anyone who isn't too thick-skinned can sense your 'don't mess with me' vibe.

Some Sexy Scenarios...
♥ Indulging your taste for hands-on danger—from the edge of a cliff top to an S&M club
♥ Exploring those hard-core fantasies (dare we say "If you dare"?)
♥ Creating your own private sex den (of course, as seedy as you like!)
♥ Worked up by erotic delay tactics

♪ I Put A Spell On You/Hurts So Good ♪

You are THE master of subtle manipulation to get what you desire. Quietly powerful and immensely resourceful, you can resort to covert methods to reach your goals. You have the determination and tenacity to never give up the chase—but only if your powerful antennae tell you that you are on the scent of your soulmate. You question (or interrogate?) others to reach the core of their personalities and underlying motives. Others usually respond to your self-reliant, enigmatic, sexy presence, so you don't actually need to do much chasing! People find your charisma devastatingly attractive, and a wise lover knows that you demand commitment and loyalty and that when they have your trust you are willing to give your all. Potential partners, who are capable of engaging with such intensity, respond by falling under your spell—yes, you know how to enslave their feelings rather than simply seduce. By keeping a shroud of mystery around your deeper feelings you attract the curious (and the brave) like a magnet. A word of advice—if a romance fails, it's important to avoid obsessive behaviour and learn to move on. This is difficult for you, as the pursuit of sexual love is often a journey into the depths of life's most intense and fascinating adventures. Partners must remember to challenge you to gain and keep your respect. If it's too easy, it just won't satisfy you.

Road to Glory/Road to Oblivion

Others should:
- hold some mystery for you; you can't resist exploring
- respect your privacy and your need to have very personal secrets
- be comfortable with lots of sex and abandon all inhibitions
- develop their perception to sense you and your needs better

Others should avoid:
- looking at anyone else—ever!
- playing psychological games at your expense
- delving too deeply into your past and personality
- questioning your loyalty and commitment

Hot dates

2000: 23 December to 14 February 2001
2001: 6 May to 3 June; 29 June to 1 August; 8 December to 18 January 2002
2002: 1 March to 13 April; 25 April to 20 May; 9 June to 7 July; 20 November to 17 January 2003

You share your Mars sign with these famous people:

Doris Day, Julie Andrews, Great Garbo, Judy Garland, Rita Hayworth, Benny Hill, Jack Nicholson, Christopher Reeve, John Travolta, Dustin Hoffman, Anne Heche, Ellen DeGeneres, Montgomery Clift, Joan Baez, Rita Mae Brown, Erykah Badu, Matthew Perry and Janis Joplin

♥♥♥♥♥♥♥♥♥♥♥♥♥♥♥♥♥♥♥♥♥♥♥♥♥

For you the adventure of love and sex must be a series of colourful opportunities. Limits are boring for you—there must be no holding back. You are excited by the thought of never repeating the same routine—and of sex not being the same twice in a row. You can be reckless, too—your idea of safe sex is remembering to lock the door before joining the mile-high club! Sexual adventure, however, is often your path to self-understanding. Those who wish to control your every move or who reveal vindictive and jealous traits will never last long with you. No matter how much you are weighed down by everyday responsibilities, you need a free rein and are more than capable of telling the world to take a hike! You are attracted to free spirits, and often to the exotic. You need an honest lover who isn't tied down by convention. In the game of love, you only play with an open hand.

Your grasp of a wide range of subjects and beliefs allows you to defend yourself with confidence and a rather superior air! Anyone who takes you on is likely to feel as though they're lucky just to get a response! Opponents may actually feel intellectually inadequate when confronted with those arrogant remarks about their judgement. Yes, you do have a tendency to take the moral high ground. You hate petty criticism or nit-picking and always fight back with relish, refusing to be put down, and intent on fighting on for your beliefs. Most of your damage is done by telling home truths in a blunt, tactless manner—you certainly take no prisoners. You rarely intend to hurt others; you simply have an irrepressible passion for the truth and refuse to be hemmed in by small-minded people.

Some Sexy Scenarios...
- ♥ studying and practising tantric sex
- ♥ being an athlete in the bedroom, too
- ♥ breaking up any journey by stopping for regular love-ins
- ♥ taking inspiration from Japanese erotic art

♪ Get It While You Can ♪

You leave potential partners with no doubt as to what you want—an exciting, joyful ride fuelled by adrenalin and sex. You exude high spirits and optimism that may prompt others to follow you to the ends of the earth (just remember the map!). Your impulse, though, may be to jump extremely quickly into relationships and then feel trapped by lovers' expectations and those humdrum responsibilities. The idea of settling down for life can be a daunting thought! Essentially you are a traveller who appreciates the journey far more than the destination. When accompanied by a kindred spirit who shares your enthusiasm and sense of fun, and who doesn't cramp your style, you'll have the freedom to explore the world and embark on sexual adventure without feeling limited by commitment. In the right climate no one is more faithful than you. No doubt you are brave enough to enjoy wild abandonment in your sex life—it will never be dull if you continue exploring and admit that you have never 'done roaming'. Your attitude to life and love is best summed up by fellow Mars (9) pioneer Janis Joplin, when she sang *Get It While You Can* and said, "Man, I'd rather have ten years of 'superhypermost' than live to be seventy sitting in some goddam chair watching TV." Right on, Janis!

Road to Glory/Road to Oblivion

Others should:
- tackle life with spontaneity and be free from burdens of expectation
- look to the future and be keen to learn anything and everything
- respect your need for freedom from clocks, chores (& even them!)
- be sporty, enjoy the outdoor life & take any opportunity to travel

Others should avoid:
- encouraging your more reckless and wasteful habits
- dampening your spirits with harsh reality and cynicism
- suffocating you with responsibilities and emotional blackmail
- taking all your promises at face value and then trying to make you keep them!

Hot dates

2000: 18 June to 7 August
2001: 14 February to 10 May; 12 July to 8 September; December
2002: 18 January to 1 March; 13 April to 14 June; 7 to 21 July; December

You share your Mars sign with these famous people:

Woody Allen, Mia Farrow, David Bowie, Brad Pitt, Marlon Brando, Noel Coward, Gerard Depardieu, Tom Selleck, George Hamilton, George Harrison, Laurence Olivier, Ronald Reagan, Roseanne, Jim Carrey, Ewan McGregor, Steven Spielberg, Julia Roberts, Jerry Seinfeld and David Geffen

♥♥♥♥♥♥♥♥♥♥♥♥♥♥♥♥♥♥♥♥♥♥♥♥

Sometimes it's a challenge for you to separate your sexual and romantic desires from your ambitions and social aspirations. The more closely intertwined they are, the more on track you feel. The goal of committed, ever-lasting love really inspires you—it's just that some of you lust after worldly achievement in equal or greater measure. So guess what? Prestige, ambition and authority in others can be effective aphrodisiacs. It's exciting for you when you are able to combine these factors in a relationship. Your partner probably needs to feel at home in an environment that is geared towards achievement and success, and to be prepared to join you on your steady climb towards material goals. Lovers must not forget that you like to be in charge—control for you is such a turn on! You know that in relationships, as in anything, hard work and dedication reap rewards. Better than most, you understand that you may not always get what you pay for, but you'll always pay for what you get!

You ask for respect and demand that you receive exactly what you're worth. That's not asking much, is it? Your steely determination and no nonsense approach mean that you suffer no fools. Those who are over-familiar, take things too lightly or who are frivolous enough not to notice your serious investment in a relationship will encounter your infamous cold shoulder and haughty indignation. You are not averse to using others rather ruthlessly IF they have proven themselves disloyal. Some of you have a chip on your shoulder from early hardship and may be trying to redress the balance. It can sometimes seem as though it's you against the world. When crossed, a less attractive instinct—'survival of the fittest'—may well come to the fore!

Some Sexy Scenarios...
♥ Exploring those master and servant fantasies
♥ Breaking the rules with sex in the boardroom after hours
♥ Enjoying the tantalisingly slow, but oh so delicious, striptease
♥ Showing your legs, easily one of your best features

♪ R.E.S.P.E.C.T. ♪

You are, of course, vigilant in your pursuit of the person who fits best into your overall plan. You approach such a task with military precision, serious intent and a sound strategy. Lovers are attracted to your discreet charm and attentiveness, and you start to see a future in a partnership when assured that your personal ambitions are not under threat. Mutual respect and integrity are paramount for you. Those who embarrass you with sexual indiscretions will feel the sudden frost bite! A romance must develop in the 'proper' manner—traditional courtship is your style and we guarantee that you are a smooth operator—possibly with a jewellery magnifier in your top pocket ready to inspect those carats! Your personal life is off-limits and you admire those who respect your privacy. If necessary, you can conduct an intimate affair for years without anyone finding out. Although you are naturally reserved and cautious in matters of love, your choice of partner might be more extrovert and daring—deep down you need someone whose experimental nature will help you discard any inhibitions. Settling for less than you deserve because of peer pressure may result in wasted years, but those born with your Mars position often discover that holding out for what they really desire secures a happiness that is built to last.

Road to Glory/Road to Oblivion

Others should:
- be in the partnership for keeps
- give you the respect and privacy you need
- leave you to organise most activities
- be young at heart, but responsible with money and future plans

Others should avoid:
- extravagance of all kinds; you hate waste
- embarrassing you in public, particularly at work functions
- being unreliable and breaking promises
- being threatened by the time you spend building your career

Hot dates

2000: 16 June to 6 August; 7 to 22 August; December
2001: January; 30 July to 14 August; 27 August to 27 October
2002: 1 March to 13 April; 28 May to 13 July; 21 July to 6 August

You share your Mars sign with these famous people:

Lauren Bacall, Matt Dillon, Farrah Fawcett, Jane Fonda, Zsa Zsa Gabor, Cary Grant, John Cleese, Alec Baldwin, Jon Bon Jovi, Brandy, Garth Brooks, Sheryl Crow, Goran Ivanisevic, Pete Sampras, Jennifer Love Hewitt, James van der Beek and Noah Wyle

♥♥♥♥♥♥♥♥♥♥♥♥♥♥♥♥♥♥♥♥♥♥♥♥♥

You are turned on by whatever is new, original and different—the wackier the better! You may enjoy (or entertain the idea of) group romps, too. Although you dislike uninvited change, you are always game for sexual experimentation to ensure that lively spark in your love life. In life and in love, you aim to shock, to rebel against authority, and to cast aside convention. You get a buzz from lovers whose attitudes are fresh and radical—never mind their status, race or creed. Better still if they share your eccentricity! The physical side of sex is not always the most important—you really stand to attention when mentally aroused. Sexual electricity is generated by your vivid fantasy world and that active imagination. Intelligence turns you on and your ideal mate will theorize about sex with you—preferably pushing back the barriers of what is considered 'acceptable'. As long as you both agree to allow each other space, it may not even matter whether you stay conventionally 'faithful' to each other.

You don't lose your temper in a personal way—ranting about life's broader inequalities is easier. It's so 'uncool' to blow your cool! When hurt, you remain self contained and detached—deafening others with your deadly silence! You react with calculated strategies and icy determination to prove your point—perhaps only striking out when your partner has been lulled into a false sense of security. You have a talent for making people feel as though their reactions are overly-emotional, irrational or stupid. You buck against any kind of restriction, and officiousness drives you crazy. You need to be a law unto yourself and must always be right. This makes you impossible to argue with! You always fight for the underdog—though secretly you admire success!

Some Sexy Scenarios...
♥ Showing your lovers that anything goes
♥ Making sure that internet stimulation transfers itself to the bedroom
♥ Sharing fantasies with your lover that will drive you both into a frenzy
♥ Abandoning yourself to the wildest passion
on the night of an electric storm

♪ I Am What I Am ♪

You never want anyone to think you're trying too hard to attract them! There's an innate reserve and pride (and fear perhaps?) when dealing with intimate one-on-one encounters. You hate overtly demonstrative behaviour and may think that showing passionate enthusiasm is a sign of losing control or getting too emotionally involved. You'd rather develop friendship first and see what develops. You are rarely the one who makes the first physical move because (secretly) you wonder if your body will match all the sexy action in your mind! Don't worry, engage the mind and the body will follow—for both of you. People may see you as impersonal, or disinterested in grabbing hold of opportunities for love. That's not actually true! Sometimes, though, that animal rights campaign seems to engage your feelings more than a weeping lover in dire distress. You will succeed in winning over your objects of desire if you develop the personal touch and show them that their flesh can turn you on just as much as their ideas! Steer yourself away from distractions and flex those mental muscles to find ways to express your physical desires. There is no doubt that you can be a most exciting and provocative lover. Get some passion for passion! When you do, you will exude an electric vibe that will attract courageous lovers for whom the only limits are those imposed by the mind.

Road to Glory/Road to Oblivion

Others should:
- keep you interested by looking to the future and its possibilities
- be cool and detached on the surface, and passionate beneath
- stimulate your mind to turn on your body
- share your goals and beliefs

Others should avoid:
- emotional blackmail, possessiveness and over-dependency
- being too conservative in attitude or in appearance
- hen-pecking and nagging
- prejudice of any kind

Hot dates

2000: 1 August to 17 September
2001: 14 August to 1 September; 21 September to 15 October; 27 October to 8 December
2002: 13 April to 28 May; 10 July to 29 August; 7 to 11 October

You share your Mars sign with these famous people:

Bo Derek, Martina Navratilova, Billie Holiday, Anthony Hopkins, Johnny Cash, Elton John, Errol Flynn, Annie Lennox, Marilyn Monroe, Tina Turner, David Copperfield, Annette Bening, Eric Clapton, Cindy Crawford, Tom Hanks, Rosie O'Donnell and Burt Reynolds

♥♥♥♥♥♥♥♥♥♥♥♥♥♥♥♥♥♥♥♥♥♥♥

You're an incurable romantic on a crusade to an amorous Shangri La. You need to experience all-embracing intimacy and complete mutual understanding. Yes, as they say, you are 'in love with love', on a quest to find the One and Only. You adore drama and the realms of role-play and fantasy, and need love to be an enactment of romantic myths full of magic and mystery. But we know that when the bubble has burst, you can also express your restless side and wish to escape. For you, it is the hope of eternal love and the merging of two souls—nothing less—that inspires you. You know that love and sex cannot be easily defined, and you have the imagination to seek an emotional and spiritual connection that goes beyond purely physical limits. Beware of the danger of becoming addicted to love—your search for experiences beyond 'ordinary life' could lead to dangerous dependencies on people or substances.

You avoid direct confrontation and can be ever so evasive. Sometimes your anger can be sublimated and your partner takes on the more antagonistic role, with you expressing passive aggression. Some may take advantage of your hyper-sensitivity and apparent vulnerability or be quick to tell you to wise up, wake up and get real. Essentially you're a dreamer who would rather not face the music, especially if it means contending with the more grim realities of life. So how do you respond? Well, when attacked or criticised, you are tempted to play the role of martyr to perfection! You also know how to whine and appear self-pitying to make others feel guilty—and it usually works! But let's not forget your innate compassion—the last thing you aim to do is cause anyone real pain.

Some Sexy Scenarios...
♥ Enjoying elaborate dressing up and role play
♥ Being inventive in your use of that celebratory champagne
♥ Remembering those erogenous zones in the soles of your feet
♥ Hiring your own love boat and taking a romantic trip out to sea

♪ Rescue Me ♪

Your search for true love is always coloured by a vision of the perfect romance. You have an innate ability to tune into your lover's thoughts and feelings, and are always prepared to empathise, support and rescue them from any peril. After all, why can't you be lover, carer, protector and redeemer in your intimate relationships? Discrimination in your choice of partners is not always your strong point. You need to avoid falling in love with an ideal, that fantasy image of the perfect relationship. Becoming a little more realistic can steer you away from involvement with those who have ulterior motives or are looking for a doormat! Beware of entering attachments because you feel obliged to save the other person from a miserable fate (or because they appear to be a guru and promise to be *your* saviour). It's frightening how quickly you could immerse yourself in another person's lifestyle and become an extension of them. You are acutely perceptive, so follow your hunches before making commitments. If you were to discover that you'd been duped and that things were not as they had originally seemed, you'd soon be off again on the trail of your real soulmate. From the outset, make sure that you know exactly what you want, and that you are using your remarkable psychic filter to weed out the unworthy. You are closer than you think to that love affair of your dreams.

Road to Glory/Road to Oblivion

Others should:
- show their sensitivity
- stay eternally romantic
- share you belief that this could be the real thing
- be strong and positive

Others should avoid:
- helping you to wallow in self-pity!
- making hurtful comments about you
- pushing you to be someone you're not
- cynical behaviour

Hot dates

2000: 31 August to 4 November
2001: 1 to 30 September; 15 October to 8 November;
8 December to 18 January 2002
2002: 28 May to 13 July; 7 August to 31 October

Days of Action
from July 2000 through December 2002

Please allow one day either side of these dates to experience the effects
* indicates that more effort will be needed to succeed in these matters today

a
+ times for: an invigorated and energetic pursuit of love and sex; strong sexual magnetism; heightened sex appeal; combining charm with assertiveness; high motivation and dynamism
- beware of: impulsive actions and overly aggressive people

b
+ times for: social fun and love/sexual adventures; taking calculated risks in love; pursuing the object of your desire; enthusiasm; grand gestures and generous displays of affection
- beware of: overestimating your chances; boastfulness; missing little details; presuming too much; hasty judgements; blowing a situation out of all proportion; becoming the sexual hedonist

c
+ times for: building solid and lasting relationship foundations; planning and strategy; concentrated effort; concrete results
- beware of: frustration; feeling restricted by rules and regulations; feeling ineffective; expressing anger internally

d
+ times for: experimenting with sexual situations; attracting creative and unusual lovers; breaking the rules of convention; pioneering social groups; perfection; uninhibited action
- beware of: a need to shock or cut off suddenly; rash moves causing irrevocable damage; reckless driving; prejudice; perverse whims; explosive encounters with unstable people

e
+ times for: defining sexual boundaries; reflection; compassion
- beware of: wearing rose-tinted glasses; laziness; hedonism; sex addiction; lack of clarity in relationships; apathy; sapped energy; sinking into a fantasy world

f
+ times for: powerful and consuming passions; increased stamina; resourcefulness; commitment; airing secret grievances
- beware of: overly-intense partnerships and desires; rage boiling below the surface; a power imbalance in a relationship; jealousy; destructive, compulsive or obsessive behaviour; brooding; sadism; victimisation

2000
8 Aug	e
29 Aug	d
*18 Sep	c
*4 Oct	f
*4 Oct	b
*22 Nov	a

2001
*1 Jan	e
*27 Jan	d
3 Feb	c
19 Feb	b
18 Mar	f
12 June	b
19 July	a
3 Oct	b
5 Nov	e
*23 Nov	a
26 Nov	d
*22 Dec	c
*30 Dec	f

2002
*28 Jan	b
*15 Mar	e
*10 Apr	d
4 May	c
8 May	f
10 May	a
3 July	b
28 July	e
24 Aug	d
*22 Sep	f
*14 Oct	c
*15 Dec	e
*28 Dec	b